The Descendant's Notebook

The Descendant's Notebook

Poems by

Kathleen Aponick

Cover design by Shay Culligan

Cover photograph by Mat Reding

ISBN: 978-1-950462-79-7

Kelsay Books Inc.

kelsaybooks.com

502 S 1040 E. A119
American Fork,Utah 84003

for Gunnel Eriksson Casey

in loving memory

Acknowledgments

My gratitude is extended to the editors of the following journals where some of the poems first appeared, sometimes as earlier versions.

Awake in the World, vol. 2 (anthology), *Riverfeet Press:* "That Week in June"

Bryant Literary Review: "The Lion at Franklin Park"

Hollins Critic: "Beached Whales"

Karamu: "Man Playing the Balalaika" as "The Balalaika"

Notre Dame Review: "Ferry Passenger"

Paterson Literary Review: from "For Judith": *Some Things I Have of Yours*

Plath Profiles: "Postscript to Sylvia"

The Listening Eye: "Guests"

The Tower Journal: "Chronicler," "Postcard from Clonown, Roscommon, Ireland," and from "Roscommon Suite": *It's a Rough-hewn Land* and *Road to the Old Village.*

The poem "Sea" appeared in *Coastal Route,* a poetry pamphlet by the author published by Feral Press and edited by John and Joan Digby.

Many thanks to my family and friends, especially to my husband Tony, for constant love, assistance, and encouragement. A special thanks goes to those who read and made suggestions on individual poems or the manuscript during its stages of development: Helena Minton, Sue Owen, Virginia McLeod, Mariève Rugo, and Tim Cremin. Tara Lynn Masih's proofreading was invaluable. And I'd be remiss if I didn't acknowledge my deep gratitude to Karen Kelsay at Kelsay Books for accepting my work and for the care she and her editors and designers applied to its publication.

Contents

I

Lost Sea Birds

Bridge Over the Charles

A hawk settled then lifted from the bridge
where my father, going home,
stopped to catch his breath,
emphysema's curse producing
utter helplessness.

And like the hawk, the indifferent river
moved on, rippling and splashing
in sea winds. Others passed:
speedboaters, bargemen, rowers
heaving against the tide

while a tour boat's passengers listened
as a guide recited a history
of the river and the land beyond—
the neighborhood where we lived.
The wind stirred, my father recovered.

After heavy rain neighbors would say,
Isn't the river high today!
For me, its fullness imparted
a buoyancy of spirit, dispelled
the grayness, though its waters,

which we waded in as children,
were forever changing: choppy,
then calm, safe, then unsafe—
like the present was to us,
erratic, so unpredictable.

Pearl Street

Its name suggests treasure—
small orbs of the sea
or Mother's pearl necklace—
not a street of small groceries,
row houses, three-deckers,
modest homes of every sort,
ours at the corner of Erie,
midway from avenue to river.

A coming and going path:
children to park or school,
parents to factories, offices,
generations off to war.
At the Blessed Sacrament
a soldier home from Vietnam
called out *My church!,* his face
lit like a sentry's back from Troy.

Shifting tides on Pearl, its surround—
families Flynn, Vasseur, Kuhn,
Donato, Brown, Seminara,
my little black friend Windmill
coming to Dana Park with friends
when I was summer counselor.
In the fifties, arrivals from the South
and Canada's Maritimes

will work in factories and presses
until they close, then move north.
In the late sixties, early seventies,
a dark turn: the age of crack.
This could be Death Row:
At Pearl Street Market a beloved
grocer was shot, a liquor store clerk
at the corner of Pearl and Franklin.

We moved to the suburbs—
the provinces as Milosz called them—
making way for other dreamers:
Brazilians, Haitians, Islanders,
all of us on a continuum,
stories vanishing but for the tales
an aunt hands down, or letters
attic drawers hide.

Land of Leaving

—for Mary Paula and Catherine

Singly or by twos and threes
in post-famine years
early relatives boarded liners
in Cobh for America
for a better life, they'd say,
a new beginning.

We went to uncover their paths,
scour farms and townlands,
unearth the striving, a longing
for the new. One told it best:
Gone for good we were.
You can't eat the grass.

They had guarded their feelings,
seldom looking back
though some returned
overwhelmed by America's chaos,
others to care for a relative
like Mother's cousin Mary Ann

whom Fortune once blessed,
delaying her return to the States
after nursing her dying father,
Patrick, of Athlone,
missing passage it seemed
on the doomed Titanic.

Sea

We were never the stars of our youth,
it was always the sea,
tales of Pegasus and hydra monsters
as real as a map's dotted wrecks.

On the Nantasket ferry we leaned
on railings to catch the mist
wondering if flung overboard
how long we'd last.

Mum heard us shrieking,
dog-paddling in roaring surf.
Don't go far! she'd shout,
her brow creased with fear.

On the Ferris Wheel, high above
Nantasket, the scene turned tame:
sky meeting sea, sea the sand, ships
mere brushstrokes on the waterline.

Today's rock and periwinkle
call back those days we floated in—
all that skyward looking,
all those drifting possibilities.

The Accident

Summer. The three of us in the yard:
I'm on the porch solving a puzzle,
my sister talking to passersby,
my brother playing with trucks in the dirt.
Everything's so alive after rain—
scent of wet soil, new leaves.

At five, workers step off the bus:
Tom Murphy, his sister, Mary,
others whose faces are all I recall.
At supper, we tell Mum of scrapes,
our triumphs in street games,
then play outdoors until dark.

Most days pass this way, unheralded.
Yet at night why do I dream
of the wave, its towering wall
poised to descend? Did it concern
my friend Patsy's mother,
the much-loved Felicia?

She was crossing Memorial Drive,
heading to her son's ballgame—
struck and killed by a motorist
sun-blinded near the overpass,
a photo of her body becoming
The Record American's page one.

Clouds spread their gray mantle
over the streets. Days fractured.
What's more: I'd ask myself,
Why am I pulling inward
when I should reach out to Patsy?
Later, I'd learn when stars implode

segments coalesce, cohere,
then move toward equilibrium.
Would knowing this have consoled me?
Tempered sorrow? For sorrow took hold
that day and those that followed,
took hold and wouldn't let go.

Lost Sea Birds

My brother Bob sends a photo from
Grandfather Ned Casey's boyhood home.
His wife, Gunnel, snapped it:
Bob between cousin Dan and his wife, Kitty,
the farm's middle-aged owners.

Kitty smiles, wind blowing her black hair
from a porcelain-like face.
She hugs a sweater round her dress,
her high rubber work boots set
deep in the rain-soaked land.

Dan's clearly a friendly type,
proud, responsible, walking cap framing
a ruddy face, his right hand akimbo,
a ragged pile of farm supplies
behind him at the ready.

It's hard to tell: Are the subjects
staring at the camera, or beyond,
toward the white-washed farm buildings,
the bleating sheep, the rusty tools
Ned must have known?

Were guests more acquainted with hosts,
not pressed for time, Bob might
have asked for stories, maybe a clue
to Ned's turbulence, how it ruled
his family, was passed on. Or of

Ned’s marriage to Minnie, of Gurranebeg,
where her father gave them half the farm
that the couple sold to strangers.
I’ll mention the fury that sparked for
Minnie’s brothers could have farmed it.

But Dan and Kitty had their own concerns.
Wasn’t all this ancient history?
After all, Ned was Dan’s granduncle,
gone long before Dan’s birth. Wasn’t it
Dan’s father, Jacob, who knew Ned?

Even if Dan knew of the old dispute
would he speak of it to distant relatives,
unsure of their intent? All that’s certain:
the subjects’ lined faces,
the slow recognition of life’s brevity.

As she clicked, Gunnel told us,
a Great Shearwater took to the wind,
flying up behind Dan and Kitty and Bob
and the green wooded grove behind the farm.
It flew out purposefully then circled back

as if Ned himself hovered,
checking to see if the townlands had changed.
Indeed, after emigrating, Ned and Minnie
often returned to Brosna and Gurranebeg.
Was it to ask for forgiveness?

After many crossings, Minnie's family
took to calling them the restless ones,
wandering souls not sure where they belonged—
They'll be lost sea birds, someone said,
forever spanning the wild Atlantic.

Guests

Mother arranged her schedule—
house family work—
those years they came to stay,

one after another:
an aunt or uncle, a cousin
out of the Navy.

They were on their own
and not liking it, wanted
a semblance of home.

Some were tied to the bottle,
others just lonely.
I need a place, we'd hear,

for a while, you know,
until I get my bearings,
until the tide turns.

We knew their rhythms,
footsteps in the hall,
on attic stairs, going out,

coming in, alone,
hating to intrude, saying:
Morning, Agnes.

Anything I can do? Chores?
Help with the children?
You just let me know.

A word, an image, a sound,
they are back, these stars
fixed in time's galaxy.

Fifteen

In navy blue uniforms,
detachable white collars,
breast pocket handkerchiefs,
starched or not,
embroidery-edged or not,
spread fanlike or not
(a chance for self-expression),
we rode the trolley
to the Mount.

Army green schoolbags
weighed us down:
books, notebooks,
last night's homework—
our translation of Cicero—
a paragraph or two,
the Latin book's
glossy cover proclaiming
the school's motto:
Labor Omnia Vincit.

Waiting on the hill: the nuns,
their struggle to impart
history's advances, retreats,
its tenuous present
(Cold War, nuclear scare).
We took tests, prayed,
learned social cues
(deference being key),
though some broke rules,
smoked in the lavs.

Beyond chapel and doctrine,
what drove us? Was it
belief in ourselves?
We strove to pass, avoid
humiliation, be accepted,
loved—like the young
in Cicero's day on the road
of longing—each of us
traveling in search of
who we might become.

Lake Ossipee

Into the wonder of white-tailed deer and Screech owls,
the scent of moist fern,
the human world intruded.

The tricks some play, the cruelty.

Perhaps the young perpetrators resented
their yearly march to scout camp.

Is that why together they exerted power they lacked
separately?

That summer's one regret:
I didn't help Johanna,

the long-braided bookish camper I met on the train
the one who didn't "fit," the one a clique
taunted with cruel remarks,
with tricks.

Why didn't I defend her, stand up, tell others?

However long ago it happened,
however more I came to know of the world,

this cowardice—
my failure to oppose intimidation—

returns, a lingering remorse,

though the beautiful Lake Ossipee
retains its wonder.

Beached Whales

We were staying in a cabin in Wellfleet,
down from the city with other arsenal families,
our fathers to fish for bass at night,
mothers and children to swim, explore

the coastal town with its salty air,
hot sand, water cooling our young bodies,
scent of a cabin's knotty pine,
backyard firs swaying in morning light.

Then someone shouted, *Beached whales!*
and we were looking down at them from cliffs.
There must have been five or six,
their mammoth bodies lined up on the sand

as if each had glided into a dock's berth.
Had they been pulled in by waves?
Trapped in the shallows at high tide
signaling one another in plaintive calls?

Later I heard their cries among the reach
of strings in a symphony by Hovhaness—
mournful, as from those aggrieved,
an elegy for the sadness of this world.

But that day in Wellfleet we could not get over
the creatures' size, could hardly believe
they were, we were told, mammals like us.
They didn't *seem* like us, we argued

but we hadn’t known their journeys,
the great crossings through the roiling Atlantic,
how intimate they were in their tightly knit groups,
as loyal and caring as we long to be.

Chronicler

—in memory of J.R.H.

Tell us again how he rode with you
where fields stretched on forever
and when you arrived at the house of your friend,
were engaged in conversation,
he ran off without you

into the woods.

You are the one who best describes what followed:
how you turned to leave only to find him missing,
how you called his name, *Rue! Rue!,*
searched woods and streams,
every marsh and field

longing for his bark—
rrrr-ruff, ruff.

I remember your concern mounted
when the sun descended and unspoken panic set in.
Was it then you promised
you'd return to search

and did, again and again.

Don't leave out the emptiness everyone felt.
Something, too, about the guilt,
what you consider even now
your betrayal of him.

Then remind us how those days led
to one you could hardly imagine
when sitting on the porch you looked up
to see him, head down, bedraggled,
about to lie a long time before you.

Today we acclaim the sheer triumph of his journey.
Was it fifty miles or more he traveled
from countryside to city?

How did he find his way? Was it
the landscape's miles of scents,
its visual cues? An inner compass
you could not have known about?

Like your mother, Joe, you have a way
with words. Our way of speaking
lacks your turn of phrase, your asides
and flourishes, that furtive glance.

Mother said you say what needs to be said—
that which carries us back
into what we cannot name.
How it would all be lost
if not for you.

II

A Life Imagined

They Were Carried

They were carried on ships
through rough seas
to this place

once marshy river edge
then wooden blocks
they occupied,

their small back yards
illuminated by starlight
that still contains them.

The Teamster's Route

—for John Hughes, in America

1900

In Cambridge, Mother's father
drives draft horses from the city barn,
steadying them as they neigh,
calming them with his touch.

Burdened with supplies,
they head to avenue loading docks,
clerks calling out, *Morning, Hughes,*
commenting on the weather.

Goods off-loaded, he signals them
to push on, prays the wagon
won't be slowed by axle break,
collision, a turn in the weather.

It's on these rides he enters
a dream reverie where
spirited beast race down
Irish hillsides, turn when he calls.

He sees the fire in their eyes,
their wild spirit—"like your own,"
a friend once told him.
And the older horses plowing fields,

they, too, fall in place,
do what he asks, as docile
as the city draft horses
he'll come to drive in Cambridge.

Past reverie, he reminds himself
why he left Athlone, garrison town
at the Irish Midlands' western edge.
Rumors have him returning home

from military service in India.
With no land, little money,
friends and relatives emigrating,
didn't he have to leave?

Noon in the city. He snaps the reins
and they return to the barn.
He'll walk the few blocks home
where Mary's waiting, the table set.

1918

His grammar schoolers—Mother and Tom—
are home for noon recess, everyone
talking about the censored letters
from the older boys, soldiers in France—

Parker carrying the wounded to makeshift
hospitals, Bill transporting supplies.
When a word suggests war's ferocity
the children stiffen in their chairs.

He's inside a silence, anxiety's constant.

1920

The boys back from the War, he's
breathing easier, life now: work,
a few words with stable owner, Fitzpatrick,
monthly Catholic Foresters meetings,

Sunday visits with the newly arrived,
sounds of the boys playing the fiddle,
mother, his youngest, the piano.
But lifting, loading, the harsh winters

render him old at sixty. Seeing the toll, Mary—
or is it one of the boys?—
arranges a new job: watchman
at the new car parts factory.

This quiet laborer, drawn to America
out of circumstance, necessity,
will carry a gun, become
a guardian of its steady progress.

1922

Death approaches. He's felled by a stroke,
the family summoned, his son Fr. Paulinus
will celebrate a Mass for the Dead.
There's the journey to Holyhood,

prayers, his mortal remains lowered
into what for him—son of Ireland,
loving husband and father—is
sacred soil of the New World.

*

What survives beyond his gun permit, these photos?

(Everyone likes the one of him walking with Mary
on Pearl Street, perhaps on their way to the Charles,
he smoking a stogie, sporting topcoat and bowler hat,
she in long black dress and cape,
a loving companionship so apparent.)

His Morris Chair graced our dining room.
It's where he read the *Boston Post,*
dozing perhaps, the past raging up—

As a child near the Shannon,
overflowing that last day,
his parents race to load the horse-drawn cart,
piling on clothes, pots, pans, mattresses.
Tempers flare. He's just a boy.
Where are they going? Why is this
happening again?

The water rises, seeps into the grasses, the road,
the cart so loaded down, so mud-stuck,
the little horse—the one he learned to ride on—
strains, forced to carry them
out of this place he loves
despite its wood-rotting dampness.

They're leaving Clonown, he's told,
going to relatives—a place he'd remember
for its crowded flats, noise, ugly scents,
no fields or horses,
no familiar riverbanks,
no views of the Shannon's boats and barges,
no riding the waves, no great clouds
to swim beneath.

Once waking from reverie,
he recalled this day they traveled by cart,
eyes closing then opening to
the sky's immensity, he wondering
what would become of them.

Wasn't he always, he'd go on asking,
both here and there, the little horse
pulling them on the uneven path,
pulling them into this other life,
this life imagined.

Postcard from Clonown

—County Roscommon, Ireland, 1999

No wonder I can't find our Hughes branch,
here where the Shannon spills over in spring,
over farms and the turf that sustained them,
their belongings soaked through and they headed
inland to relatives with troubles of their own.

First House in the New World

—to a young relative

Mother lived here as a child,
her family's layered in the brown
shingles, not that locked fence
waiting for the house to sell.

To sit on that porch, her parents
crossed an ocean, lived in rooms
south of here, worked long hours,
saved their pennies.

In this 1920 photo, her father—
elbow on the railing, hand cradling
his head—looks toward us,
his descendants, never to know us,

though he'd recognize our names,
certain gestures, ways of glancing,
a penchant to roam, reluctant
to be corralled, defined.

The yard, like their words and acts,
is a ghost-weed thicket. Letters
we've found hint at dreams
harbored, a yearning to matter.

Still, so much is missing
as if gale force winds banished
any trace of their passions—
shouts of pain or joy.

If only we had their stories,
recited them over and over,
jotted them down to tell us
who they were—who we are.

In a Time of Great Disorder

On a wharf's grassy hill
a segment of an iron chain
lay opposite the Custom House
where Hawthorne clerked:

separation under pressure,
yanked from a solid mooring.

Hawthorne's Hester Prynne knew this,
cast out by society's strictures,
taken from all she knew,
all she might have cared about.

Those today fleeing war and tyranny
know this kind of rupture.

Of their fate at the mercy of others
some seem not to care.

If pulled from what we know
pray we meet with those who do,
that we have the will to start again
in a land so foreign.

Ferry Passenger

—imagined for a cousin, Tim Reilly, who died September 11, 2001,
North Tower, World Trade Center

We boarded for the crossing that day,
quiet, trembling, not looking back,
never imagining, not in our wildest dreams,
you were among the missing.

It has been ages since we abandoned the gods.
Forgive us but they came to seem
separate and remote from us,
responding to another age.

Yet had we known your fate that day
and that of the others, known, too,
of Achelous—patron deity
of the "silver swirling" Achelous,

the largest river in Greece—
we would have suspended disbelief,
yes, flung it into the cold water,
intoned the gods, implored Achelous

to save you and the others
that day where you worked in the city,
that day when the towers fell.
Perhaps it would have mattered.

Roscommon Suite

Bealnamulla

Mother said her mother came from Bealnamulla.
We loved to say it—Beal na mew la—
from the Irish *Beal Atha na Muille,*
meaning *mouth of the mill ford.*

In Bealnamulla, of wider Athlone,
the family lived in Rooskey—
Ruscaigh in earlier times for its bogs and swamps,
meaning, in effect, hard to farm.

Government-bestowed, the land went to ancestors
dispossessed, as those before them were
who labored long as tenants,
deserved what was theirs.

Legend has it the early ones looked skyward
with such weariness a spell was cast.
Their descendant, I dream of them carried off
by mute swans flying over Bealnamulla,

the creatures' powerful wings propelling them
forward, lifting them over vales and wheat fields,
away from their labors, toward the banks
of Lough Rynn, toward freedom.

On the day Grandmother left—
was her father, Michael, cutting peat from the bog,
his mind on work, or his daughter Mary leaving?
Did Mary prepare tea for her mother, Bridget?
Or Bridget serve Mary?

No doubt there was tension: questions
from Mary's sisters, Bridie and Katy
(the whys, the wherefores),
the teakettle singing
Mary's going, Mary's going.

A long time denied—stasis—then a shift.
No!—more a quake, villages emptying out,
thousands emigrating, those left behind
keeping company with God's silence.

It's a Rough-hewn Land

It's a rough-hewn land, a few hills remaining.
Cousin Jimmy stops to show us the bog.
It's where he cuts the peat—
soil of wetlands and old forests—
in the shape of bricks.

The house is modest, white-framed,
set on a rise of rolling hills.
There's energy, movement,
though not enough for Jimmy's teens
eyeing our shiny rental car.

Jimmy's wife Mary shows us
rooms where they dine and sleep
and I wonder what they think of us:
distant relatives they hardly know
looking for our past in their present.

We ask where our grandmother lived.
Jimmy points to a thatched-roof cottage
leaning into the hollow, a refuge
for travelers, he says, escaping
high winds, driving snow.

Our grandmother knew those winds
turning today's clotheslined sheets
into whirling dervishes, knew
the dirt floors stacked with farm tools,
grains, root vegetables.

Somewhere—no, everywhere in this place—
I know she dreamed another life.
Later, on a hill with Jimmy,
we survey the land's rough beauty,
the great treeless distance—

what she saw pulling up turnips,
potatoes, tending animals.
At night, as she waited for sleep,
I hope the windows filling with stars
braced her for what followed.

Road to the Old Village

> *"They called it Primrose Alley for the hedges that bloomed along the roadsides."*
> *—Jimmy Lennon*

We were asking him where the road went,
the one by the field where he stood
watering the cows.

I can't leave now, he said, *Chris will take you.*

And as we walked, Chris led us on his bike
into an overgrown vale—site of
abandoned nineteenth-century homes,
hedges, vines, plantings gone wild.
Past fallow plots, once farms, now a sea
of green and wheat-colored grasses,
old boundaries set off by rusty wire fences.

There were three farms, Chris reported,
two owned by bachelors.

I scanned the family graph in my mind,
recalling the fate of relatives there.
One, Willie Fury, was disabled,
injured, I recall his grandniece saying,
by the Black and Tans,
who often targeted innocents
in the war for independence.

Still, that day was a scene of motion,
of sound—the faintest brush of leaves
flickering, a swish of blowing grasses,
the blackbird's sharp caw,
everything cast under billowing clouds
as in a painting by Constable or Jack Yeats
should either have wandered in
to record that day.

Side Trip to Ballylee

We climbed the tower at Ballylee—
Thoor Ballylee, in Gort,
summer home to Yeats and Georgina,
young Ann and Michael.

A spiral staircase led us up
(I was with my sister and niece)
past rooms where they gathered
or waited out a storm.

It's a square-shaped Norman tower,
a rock-carved fortress, wrought
like his stanzas, measured
like his thoughts: structures pressed

with word-mortar into lines—
expressions of love and loss:
for friends, his beloved,
a nation fractured by ancient rifts.

Through a slit in an outer wall
we spied summer's awed glory,
not as relatives of the tower's builders,
a family of wealth and stature,

but as descendants of those who fell
on hard times, boarded ships,
crossed an ocean. We stood
where he stood who never knew them,

he who recorded stories of their
heroes, saints, and warriors,
myths and journey-tales they carried
with them into other worlds.

Then we turned, as they must have—
Yeats and Georgie in their time—
toward a room where embers warm
on cool summer days.

We listened as they spoke,
he about a word, a title, she
whether unity's achieved,
the meaning glass-clear.

We tried but couldn't imagine
what transpired centuries ago
in the shade-filled woods below us,
or on nearby paths and fields.

Nor at other sites we visited
where early relatives went on
yearning for a new life
on some Blessed Isle.

The Stars That Form Auriga

I saw them again,
the stars that form Auriga
so visible on a night like this.
My father and his father,
my mother and her mother,
ancestry common, uncommon,
walked out under these stars.
Perhaps there was laughter
or singing, or someone spoke
words of unparalleled beauty
which the night air dispersed.
So much has occurred
I must set it down, at least
a small part of what's recalled
though much will be lost.

III

Landscapes and Elegies

Persist

Evergreens unfold their wrapped cones
while neighborhood children
jostle one another
waiting for the school bus
in this quiet suburb.

Far off in time, I left my house in the city,
rushed by two elms, witnesses
to the family's unsettled past
though I welcomed their shade,
the breeze through my window.

Only now do I see how those trees instruct:
woody rings, gnarled bark,
bird-nesting boughs, all withstanding
ice, drought, lightning,
every fierce impediment.

Massachusetts Green

Shrugging off melancholy,
I notice the green around me,
its power to renew.
It's in washed spring lawns,
aspens trembling before rain,
rock-clinging lichens.

Along the riverbank
where crabgrass and clover
run rampant and willows rustle,
a boy watches his kite
sailing off, into oblivion.

On the state's western side,
what catches my eye in Hawley—
fields of yellow-green corn tassels,
farm stands of zucchini,
green peppers, kale, lettuce,
various herbs.

City greens hold their own:
boxwood hedges lining fences,
cedars (the scent of them!) marking
property lines. Given the season,
the circumstance, door wreathes
decorate or mourn.

Other greens signaling loss—
moss on Concord gravestones,
a cross by a highway,
a passing soldier's fatigues,
leaf-covered battlefields
we walk on, unaware.

Summers in the bird sanctuary
lift my spirit when hydrangeas'
pale green blossoms
look out at me, sharp contrast
to the branches, the rough
bark of oaks and pines.

In nearby forests, you'll see
grapevines colonists harvested
centuries ago. I often wonder
what names local Indians gave
the kettle hole's floating lily pad
with its saucer-sized leaves,

or other forest greens of
varied shades and textures—
trailing arbutus, ferns, Solomon Seal,
wintergreen, a spread of mayflowers'
shiny leaves, the transparent
wings of a dragonfly.

I don't ignore green's warnings—
poison ivy's three-leafed scourge,
for one, or its cousin poison oak
whose calling cards rash and fever
assailed me in Brewster.
Once, while wading through

floating seagrass off Gloucester,
I noticed kelp's sinuous dance,
how the surf's cold green bands
numbed my skin. Late July,
at Crane Beach in Ipswich,
greenheads sting.

On the Cape's bayside
where the water's warmer, the air
more diffuse, green's subtler,
though the hearty scrub pines,
profuse in these parts,
wear the darkest green.

Don't be afraid, I tell myself
when the blues invade, watch
how green adapts. See its changing
shades in the salt marshes,
in the Great Marsh itself
stretching its large maternal shawl
north from Cape Ann to Salisbury.

Two Photos

I'm thirteen. Graduation's over,
my limp hair mirroring a lowering spirit,
a cloud-filled June's mugginess.
I walk to my parents waiting for me
in front of the old funeral parlor,
a rare moment for they were seldom together.

I ask if I could take their picture,
the one you're holding: Tim and Agnes,
side by side, together, yet apart,
his once black hair now a steely gray,
the pants of his double-breasted suit
dipping below a beer-widened waist,

she in her navy suit and pill box hat
in keeping with that era's style,
white gloves draped across her purse.
They both seem happy, relaxed.
I wonder if that's to please me.
I snap the photo. If I could

go back and rearrange their future,
soften the way it turned out,
the two of them like lions,
captives of one another,
clashing in a war of words
though seldom in front of us.

But that day is different—
my aunt and cousins at the house
to celebrate the occasion,
their presence distracting me
from the gloom I feel,
a growing despondency.

After sandwiches and ginger ale,
cake and ice cream in the dining room,
someone snaps this next photo:
Smiling family with dog.
I suppose it's like other photos
hiding what lies beneath.

After my father leaves
(I'm not sure where he is going),
talk centers on news of the day,
my plans for high school,
stories about other relatives,
how their lives are going.

I remember listening, not talking,
feeling strangely absent.
There was the sound of talk,
glasses clinking, someone laughing.
It was such a humid day.
I couldn't wait for the rain.

Woman and Young Girl, ca. 1890

—on an unidentified photo by Charles Henry Newman

I found it in the town archives—
this photo of a seated woman
with a bible on her lap,
a daughter by her side—
or is this a grandchild?

It's hard to tell their mood,
how they regard one another
for serious expressions—
preferred in that age—
hide any sense of affection.

I like to think there was joy:
a love-filled marriage, praise
for a sampler's clever stitches,
curiosity about the world,
friends they'd laugh with, rely on.

Notice the road behind them,
the one interrupting a field,
a road they surely took
on errands, to school or church.
Or perhaps in dreams

fleeing conformity, rushing
along the path time and again
craving a route to freedom
miles from the order and manners
that held them hostage.

Air

These rainy days remind me of Bavaria,
the valley where I taught in the sixties.
When the rain stopped, my friend Linda
often drove us from school to countryside
through miles of lush hill farms. We were
heading for a restaurant on the River Main,
breathing in scents of terraced vineyards.

*

Before his death my father caught his breath
in a medicated atomizer's compressed air.
Without it once, I saw him clutch the fence,
his emphysemic lungs struggling for air.
In Halloween's woodsmoke, a funeral parlor's
mums seemed his quick short breaths,
tall red glads bursts of his heart's blood.

*

I love sea air. As a child, I'd lean from
boats to catch the spray mist of waves.
In Bavaria, I learned of another mist—
not the Valley's but in towns a world away,
napalm's mist raining down on the land,
on transferred fathers of children I taught,
on the beautiful people of the East.

*

My mother often said, *Kathleen, why not*
take a walk; don't stay in on a day like today.
I once felt faint in an airless church,
rushed to a fire escape landing, breathed in
welcoming scents of lilacs, a nearby magnolia.
Lent's incense or a May altar's roses
could hold me captive, color my mood.

*

As I bend to weed the garden, the herbs
are a paradise of air: woody thyme,
basil, marjoram, parsley, peppermint.
My life sign is air, my husband's, too.
It was my mother's when she lived.
It's in our history, its power recalling
what frees, what confines.

Cathedrals

At first they seem too grand,
too enormous to feel part of,

that sense you have at a waterfall's
roar or a mountain precipice.

Yet nearing one in fog today
something of its spirit lifted me

from winter's bleakness,
a sadness I felt about my life.

Monet says changing air and light
give objects their real beauty

as when light illuminates burnished
wood or a stained glass bible scene.

As a child, I'd found promise
in the skylights, the vaulted lofts,

the sculptured saints and stone-carved
angels blowing hymns skyward,

though some images frightened—
the exterior's flying buttresses

and those gargoyles out of whose mouths
rain pours its torrents. Mistakenly,

I thought burning incense signified
our ashes, not prayers rising to heaven.

It must have been the faith I had
then that enveloped me, cast

its wide protective net around
my young life, just beginning.

On Memorial Day

Mother often took us to the cemetery
on Memorial Day. Wandering off,
we'd read the names and dates
etched on gravestones,
brief notes—*child died in infancy,*
son fallen in the War. . .

Before her family's grave,
Mother set geraniums to honor her parents,
soldier-brothers of World War I,
her nephew—a World War II
Navy veteran who died at thirty-eight,
wounded in the heart.

Heads bowed, we said a silent prayer
which was our tradition,
everyone reflecting in his or her way
what the departed meant to them
though Mother knew them all,
knew them best.

Leaving the cemetery, I'd think:
Perhaps *our* names will appear on stones
like these, people driving by like we do
wondering, if only for a moment,
who we were, what we did in this world
that still holds endless wars.

Adrift

—in memory of R.E.H. (1926-1964)

Whenever winds move through
brushing against rock jetties
I think of you and your years at sea.
Kind, soft-spoken cousin,
returning to us on leave,
we saw you weave, inebriated,
sensed an endless sadness
though we were young and didn't
understand the whole of it.

Moving from California as a teen
after your parents' divorce
in the years before our births,
you became the attic dweller,
studied high school mechanics,
joined the Merchant Marines.
Sea bound, did you feel freedom,
no one hovering?

Mustering out, you returned to California
and when the War drew America in,
you stepped forward, signed up.
For your valor in the Pacific,
you were honored: We found
your medals in attic bureaus.
If only you kept a log, sent letters,
we'd have your thoughts.

Back in Cambridge with Mother
ill winds turned favorable:
You were in the new Air Force,
assigned as radio repairman.
It seemed a fresh start.
Yet in a year, you're discharged—
for medical reasons, records state.

Dear cousin,
you never lost your mooring,
there was never a mooring for you.
In your troubled state, this downward slide,
you knew you couldn't stay with us,
Mother having challenges of her own.
So rooming houses became your home.

We loved the attention you showered on us,
kind acts helping Mother with chores—
painting, wallpapering, hoisting up
storm windows in the fall.
But the sea monster, Self-destruct,
had set his sights on you,
would swallow you whole.

In the ocean we flail in,
your blue eyes keep searching ours.
What are they searching for?
Hearing your voice say my name
you appear, a lone mariner
forever heading out to sea.

For Judith

—a friend and former colleague

Seismic

After waitressing on the Cape that summer,
we began our years of teaching,
afternoon stillness welcoming us home
from Cambridge schoolrooms.

Then that day in November, bell-clear—
the principal sending radio news
over the intercom, confusing at first,
then startling, wrenching:

Governor Connolly's been shot, the President. . .
the first lady. . . reaching for him. . .
Sounds, commotion, the children in line
to go home unaware, chatting away.

You shook hands with him at a Worcester parade.
I canvassed neighborhoods in the campaign,
made calls. *Surely he'll survive*, you insisted.
Then, hesitating, *The news will turn, won't it?*

For we could not imagine a future without him,
compose its narrative. After coffee at Hayes Bick's,
you caught the bus to Brighton, I to Mother's
to read tributes, watch T.V.'s awful footage.

That fall held other portents: One evening
we opened the door to steam, the kitchen in ruins,
hissing radiators, paint peeling down
like top-heavy fronds.

Perhaps it was a sign before the full dissolve:
Your plans to marry, my father's sudden death.
Up ahead, the sixties accelerant-lit.
But that decade's first years—

their youthful excitement, endless summers
before that seismic shift, fixed in time—
a dream incongruous, surreal, a tape
replaying down through the years.

Some Things I Have of Yours

Passing townspeople retreating into large colonials,
apartments whose red brick softens
in New England's slanting light,
I remembered some things
I have of yours:

Two children's books by Milne, inscribed in your hand
(gifts for grandchildren if you have them);
your oar painting of a fisherman
straining in rough Atlantic waves,
pushing as we did against the tide.

And from that sunlit time before your marriage ended
the wooden crib you lent for Mike.
It leans against a cellar wall, its prancing lamb decals
oblivious to threats like high winds
shaking the windows, downing the apples.

Our pupils offered apples. Remember how they set them
on our desks in fall? It was a time
we believed a life was ruled by fate,
always some outside force,
never our faulty natures.

In recurrent dreams, those students line up
to come in, not to us half-formed
in our early twenties but to the Oracle
who prepares them for loss.
But will they take heed?
Will they listen?

That Week in June

It began with squalls
then the sky turned azure blue.
I was in and out of what I needed
to do when a friend called to say
a plane was missing: a neighbor
with his young son, Chris,
on their way to the Sound
to fish and water ski.

Media is everywhere, she warned.
For now, let's say nothing.

Once, Chris came to my teacher's
desk to have homework corrected,
to my door with his sister Sara
Halloween nights for trick-or-treat,
their mother, Joanne, steady guardian,
watching at lawn's edge.
We crowded into her family room
to offer support, watch coverage,
hear a news anchor's report:

If they survived the impact,
found a cove. . .

All this, as late spring held forth,
distracting us with life's blossoming:
rhododendrons by the house,
yards of fragrant magnolias,
the beginnings of pears,
teens in swim gear headed
for the pond, some to ballfields.
At a briefing, the fire captain spoke:

No doubt the plane drifts in the tides,
a mesh of weeds. All we can do is wait.

Spring returns with its beguiling mask
as if nothing unsettling happened.
The trees go on budding.
The commuter train arrives at the depot.
We take our daily walks.

Note to Emily

—Since I have no sweet flower to send you, I enclose my heart.
—E. Dickinson, from a letter, 1858

I've read plans are moving ahead
to restore your garden.
Flowers you grew and gave as gifts—
asters, lilies, yarrow, buttercups—
like those in fields they carried you over
to your grave—will resume their place,
like actors returning to the stage
after long absence.

Herbs and old hedges will reappear,
a honeysuckle arbor to perfume the air.
I'll be looking for your grape trellises,
Greville roses and marigolds,
daffodils, hyacinths, chrysanthemums.
A greenhouse will house the ferns,
the gardenias and fuchsia, the heliotropes.

As then, Emily, the world beyond lapses,
slips into this strange delirium.
Hot spots are like flares seen from space.
We can't pull away from the suffering,
constant war, its consequences—
though we know even a garden
has its dramas, its hostile takeovers,
diseases, adaptations.

It’s true there’ve been advances, amazing
in their breadth. In gardening
better knowledge of the soil, ways to treat
the common weed. But too often
efforts for human understanding,
herculean on the part of some, fail.
Like you we wait, at times consoled
finding beauty and wonder where we can.

Postscript to Sylvia

You didn't know us.
We entered Poetry's portal after you,
sharing coffee and drafts of poems
at kitchen tables, in drafty classrooms.
Books, too, some by those you knew.
Lowell and Sexton were two.

Formalism instructed you.
Our teachers were its students.
Like them, we studied it, then fled its strictures.
Hadn't you borrowed the Academy's metrics
from masters? Shakespeare, for one,
full fathom five thy father lies.

Others, too, left their mark:
Thomas and Roethke, surely Ted.
You caught their sounds and rhythms.
Soon life had you shouting to the gods
in *your* style, *your* lyrics,
intense and true.

Stars flame, recede: The Muse can be cruel.
You grew out of fashion:
Some mimicked you.
Others scorned and mocked
though never equaled the best
of your clear-as-a-bell lines.

If you could have lingered—
fled with the children from that cold London flat,
found haven, stood your ground, but you were
sicker than they knew, the mind's circuits
unattended, flying off course,
no one there to set them right,
no one there but you.

River Force

—in memory of Paddy O'Brien, b. abt. 1786, Co. Kerry, Ireland

It may have been fall's Samhain
or a local saint's day—five farmers
celebrating at the pub, a bodrum
playing songs of love and rebellion,
glasses lifted high in toasts
before setting off for home.

At the river they'd decide:
Walk the long way to the bridge
or swim across, there at the banks.
Strong Kerry men, they often swam
the Brown Flesk, swollen that day,
coursing after heavy rain.

When one asked loudly,
Are we up for the challenge?
all slipped in knowing
a day of swirling gusts meant
strong limbs were needed
to outwit the tidal pull.

Was it the river's demonic spirit
that caught one in the riptide?
His friends swam furiously to save him,
calling out to each other, *Paddy! Conor!*
Tim! Hang on, Dan! Yet each
was pulled down in turn,
into the water's fierce vortex

recalling for me an incident close by—
not from a river raging but frozen:
five boys on New England's Merrimack
a decade ago—four linking arms
to rescue a fifth on ice breaking up,
all perishing. Any river freeze
stirs the memory, cuts deep.

On that day in Killeentierna,
Paddy and the others, in their prime,
were as helpless. Nature deceives.
Like insects to a flytrap, we enter
its promise, think we know it,
trust ourselves, take the risk.

There may be faint memory of the men
where the Brown Flesk flows.
No sign marks where they'd hoped
to cross. There's only the descendants'
awe, their sorrowful wonder discovering
an ancestor lost to river force.

IV

The Racing Heart

Late February

It was a time of snow and cold,
ice blocking driveways,
snowdrift mounds tall as hillsides.
We felt marooned, forgotten.

Yet we knew the siege would end
when the earth around us
warmed and the sky turned
azure blue. To go forward

we needed to believe this
so that later, as we walked down
a sunlit road, wind at our backs,
breathing in earth's sweet soil,

attuned to forsythia's yellow
light, the whistling trees,
we would be silently grateful
for the moment we were in.

The Bear

On a trail near Banff, we split up,
you to scale the high path,
I, to skirt the lake's edge
canopied by fir and spruce.

Haunting calls of loons echo
across the water. A woman passes,
warns of a bear. Calm at first,
I'm soon forced to slow the mind,

loosen fear's grip, try reason:
Weren't most bears harmless?
Hadn't the park video explained
what to do if confronted?

Yet in this world of no exits,
a racing heart has a mind of its own,
takes me to the brink, explodes
its confusion in my ear.

If only I could remove myself,
upend reality. A thud in the brush.
I turn, sense the bear's presence,
hear it roar. It has seen me.

Keep going, the heart drums.
And I am a child again running
from terror: Jake, a wizened, angry man
in black attire, stamping his cane

on Pearl Street, raging at the world
and at me at seven passing him,
running a city block to my door,
the locked door behind which

no one hears me scream, or fall
in exhaustion waiting to be saved,
to be pulled up by a loving hand
which never comes.

Fear and terror: real, assailing,
taking shape in the landscape:
the dark nature of the world
leaping in a bear's fury.

Seen

Was that you I saw in the Square
waiting to cross the street?
I wanted to say hello
but the light turned to Walk,
the crowd was moving.

Rebel, scholar, cynic, mistrusting
all things establishment,
you loved history's drama,
the inexhaustible tales.
Being caustic, scornful of elites,

you seemed idol-less yet there were
two you held in high esteem.
Van Gogh's portrait hung
in your rented room. Like him,
you knew the mind's collapse.

And in that *Newsweek* photo of you
leaving the Yard,
you have the air of RFK.
His politics were yours,
his rough ebullience.

After the president's death,
King's, RFK's, everything changed.
I'd found another; we parted,
the stars for us misaligned.
Had we spoken that day in the Square

I might have asked how you were,
if the years had been kind
yet how empty the words
would have seemed,
how hollow and pointless.

Vise

—in memory of Jane Bell

You crossed the lawn,
hurrying to sit in my kitchen,
saying *I'll only stay a minute.*
And we talked, you of John,
the children, everything
moving in a rush, *much to do*
at home, at your job
rescuing those in crisis.

Before John called to say
you took your life,
why hadn't I sensed
distress in your voice,
known of your despair?
I should have listened,
should have spoken,
should have. . .

It was hormonal, he said.
You were hospitalized but left,
they couldn't keep you
in those haunted wards,
nor tame the behemoth
terror that seized those
you sought to help,
then you.

Days passed before they found you
in a locked garage in Peabody,
a letter of regret by your side.
Depression was a sentence
you could not endure,
would not survive.
Was there no other way?
No antidote, no salve?

Tough city girl, why did you
let this difficult world
lean on you this way,
press you in its vise?
In all those years,
you seemed the strong one,
someone who could have
pulled out, pushed back.

When I pass through Cape Ann,
drive by your house,
I think of you, visits roaming
the shore with the children,
suppers with greens from the garden,
sharing drinks, hearing
your North Shore stories,
the latest gossip.

A woman enters my yard.
She is you, Jane, that day
of shifting clouds, air electric
with your nervous excitement,
my mind oblivious to the signs,
the fragile underpinnings.

Witness

—for Anna Ahkmatova (1889-1966)

I arrived long after the war.
It was a month after your death.
From the window of the hotel
I saw snow fall like white ash,
fall on streets wide as rivers.
It swirled up, each flake a soul,
each soul not wanting to settle.

I had not known of you then,
how history's maelstrom caught you
in its wide spiraling current,
had not read your stark responses
to the edicts, known you memorized
what you wrote to save it,
stayed when others left.

On a tour bus near the Winter Palace
I faced a barren, treeless square.
No sign of life, the palace
like a cake, its frosting tinted green,
edged in white, the surround
scrubbed clean of loss and suffering,
the bloody past.

In the Armor Room of the Hermitage
we filed past breastplates,
helmets, swords: a sampling
of war's killing tools. Outside,
by the Neva, we paused,
as you must have, Anna,
needing the river's solace.

On the ride back to Moscow,
the sun, low on the horizon, blazed
as if spring would not release
the thought of you. Beside us,
birches relaxed after a freeze.
I thought of foot soldiers
stumbling home from the front.

Was it in deference to you no leaf stirred?
You had stayed through the terror:
its threats, intimidations, waited
at the prison gates for months to see Lev,
charged as an enemy of the State—
or was it for being your son?

Yet years earlier, parenthood it seems
was not for you, nor Nikolay,
freedom from obligation your preference.
Giving Lev to Nikolay's parents to raise
exacted a price: The strain between you grew.
For years, you would try in vain
to recover his love.

The Muse was more forgiving.
Taunted by authorities,
rejected by the inner circle,
you went on writing. Only later
would the public discover
these truth-telling lyrics,
feel the light of your words—

a constellation’s steady gaze
fixed on what happened,
bearing witness to the age.
How passionate the poems still are, Anna.
How exposed you were.
How fearless.

Man Playing the Balalaika

You were walking the beach at Yalta,
smoking, alone, beckoning to us
in a woolen cap, clothes too flimsy
for the cold spring air.
Were you a laborer on holiday?
You seemed old, though this photo
shows you'd be no more than fifty.
When we said we were teachers
from America's posts in Germany,
you looked down, saying something—
prisoner or *prisoner of war.*

Turning back, you spied the balalaika
I'd bought at the tourist shop.
We coaxed you to play. Was it a folk
song? A dance? The sounds were
so light and fast on the stony beach,
the sky behind you a whiteness,
the sea to our backs, calm, flat
as if readying for the stir
the racing strings would make.

You could have been Orpheus,
mesmerizing us with his lyre
but we were far from the Greek isles,
the gods there still reeling
from war's savagery.
As then, music casts its spell.
Had it for you once—a soldier
singing with comrades,
breaking for a moment
from war's cruelty?

For when the music turned high-pitched,
as intense as a hundred guitars
rushing with a dance-like tune,
I saw the prison inside you dissolve,
the bars severed by music's pull,
gates swinging open as from a gust,
and everyone—the dead and the living—
dancing out over the land.

Afternoon of the Snapping Turtle

The day it appeared
rain moved daily on the field,
on asters and delicate Queen Anne's lace.
Horse nettle and black-eyed Susans
nodded with the weight of it
as blades of grass arched like penitent sinners.
Ancient creature from the netherworld,
it had pulled itself from an overflowing swamp,
plodded along like the long wet days
when boys in their slickers,
in their green ignorance, started taunting it,
repelled and intrigued by its strangeness,
its medieval slowness. And then
it charged, reared its head, waved
its tail in defiance until the frightened boys
saw themselves in its struggle,
caught their shame in the solemnity of its eyes.
Now, near a rock of its color, only its tracks
are erased by never-ending rain
when the boys come back to talk of it.

Small Frying Pan

He flung it though I didn't see his arms move
just the pan as it ripped past,
just his head turning as each of ours turned
that afternoon.

Why? Was it someone's gesture,
someone's tone? Why can't I recall?

He was at the stove frying eggs
in the pan we used for quick meals.
And then it was a gauntlet, the metal handle
propelled outward, flying.

We crouched down, heard the pan
hit the wall, the wall he'd painted
in a hopeful time, a time
he must have felt at peace.

Only after the crashing sound,
in the silence of it, could we separate
from his rage, could our minds
move beyond the scene, beyond him.

And then I thought how strange it was
to worry about the pan, misshapen on the floor,
whether it could ever be used again.
And the wall with its slight dent.

Why was I focused on these things?

One of us moved and soon we were
back in our assigned parts, unnerved
yet only slightly, the pan and wall changed,
not much of anything else.

View from the Outside

—in memory Louis Brown, age 15

When I read of your death,
snow was falling here in the suburbs
as it had the night before
in the city where you lived,

falling where your young body lay
in jeans, a high school jacket's
satin sheen, hi-tops, your cap's X
saluting Malcom.

At first you were nameless,
another city youth caught
in the crossfire.
I could only imagine you
as the others before you.

Soon you were revealed:
Louis Brown of Dorchester.
I saw your face, learned you were
a youth leader on your way
to a meeting that night—

Urban Youth Against Violence.

All you wanted—truce among brothers,
accommodation among the gangs.

How do we disable the violence engine
ripping dreams apart? Yours
for college while working two jobs.
What else had you dreamed?

At New Testament Pentecostal
a vigil was held in your honor,
scores there to remember you.
Your stepfather spoke:

His death was not in vain, he insisted.
It will be a cause to unify us
into action.

We cannot go back, Louis,
to that corner where you fell
in undeclared warfare,

cannot deflect the bullet
nor diffuse the shooter's anger,
the confusion of his life.

Death won't be undone
nor the terrible void
your absence created.
We must be moved, Louis,
moved to action.

The Lion at Franklin Park

We observe you in sunlight, golden offering
on a sculptured mound, blinking,
throwing back your head to shake off annoyances.
Do you avert your eyes to ignore us?

What has memory imprinted on you
in cages where you paced in maddening circles?
Games of life and death in the Coliseum, in circus tents?
How cavalierly we have used you.

Loyal companion, marrying for life, symbol of bravery,
your image decorates ancient palaces, family crests.
You are prized in statuary. With your seated twin,
your noble presence guards our library.

Seeing you stare beyond us and the dizzying moat
how can we not wonder of your dreams—
forest fern, monkey hoot, bird screech.
In such confines, what would we dream?

On California Street

—for Tony

Driving by our first apartment,
the two-floor duplex in Newton,
I remember the girls upstairs,
their boyfriends coming and going,
cars in the driveway blocking ours.

You traveled to work on 128.
I caught the bus to my Boston job.
Fridays, the work behind us,
a radio played *Jazz in the Evening*.
We had dinner, unwound.

Thinking back, didn't friends nearby
seem to have it all—house of their own,
children, a dog, Cape Cod vacations?
They called us lucky singles, envied
our freedom though we envied them.

Those two years now seem idyllic:
walks by the Charles, friends in for dinners,
family gatherings. You built
model ships, I learned rug making,
wrote poems for an evening workshop.

All this before the move north,
our friends' quarrels, their split.
Then the adoption. Everything
to come that would test us dearly
but never break us.

Storm Fears

Fall approaches. I watch you cut down
a pear tree split by storms.
It had seemed invincible but now
lies like a wounded soldier
as bees it hosted, trying hard to hold on,
scatter, fly off to build new nests.

Once, with electricity out, a transistor radio
kept us in touch with the outside world:
Soviet Republics declaring independence
from a State they never felt part of,
breakaways severing ties to remain intact
to keep a sense of who they are.

I think I have asked too much of you
through my illnesses and failures.
Tensions rise. We beat them back, cling together
seeing the better nature of one another.
Perhaps fearing what it would mean
to be pulled apart.

Souvenir

It's a toy birch canoe
bought on a childhood
trip to Nantasket.

Mother brought us there
hot summer days
to swim the cold Atlantic.

Dusty, its paddles missing,
I can't discard it, can't
throw out Paragon Park's

whirling merry-go-round,
its roller coaster terror,
the Pavilion's ocean breeze.

Nor forget the native tribes
I'd read about—the Massachusett,
the Wampanoag.

They'd fished the peninsula's
quiet lakes and island ponds,
centuries earlier

chased down enemies,
or were themselves pursued
in brutal raids—ghost figures,

yet so much like us
thwarted by violence and war
in the briefness of their stay.

Osprey

—off the Maine coast

When our tour boat headed into the narrows
from the riverway, away from the cold
ocean winds, we saw them above us
conferring in twos and threes.

They were like the birds of dreams,
brown-feathered with patches of
white beneath their wings. When
someone called *Fish hawks! Osprey!*

one fell, dove past us in a free fall,
feet first into the water, its fierce talons
tightening on an unsuspecting menhaden
betrayed by its iridescence.

And as we ploughed through the narrows—
called Hell's Gate for its shifting bends,
the deceptive shallowness near the banks—
the bird, lord of the air, rose again.

The guide signaled to look shoreward
to a well-known resident's cottage
but my eye stayed with the bird
growing indistinguishable from the pines.

At home, I imagine it in a moment's passing,
see it fishing the narrows or nesting,
wings folding into that relaxed alertness
of birds preparing to sleep.

At other times, it follows the tour boat path
as it had that afternoon summers ago,
gathering strength from the flock,
disappearing at will.

There was such a biting wind on the deck
that day, the birds such wild spirits
maneuvering the air, echoing
a longing I still can’t name.

Notes

The poem "Lost Sea Birds" draws from a photo, family lore, and a trip my brother Bob Casey and his wife Gunnel made in 1977 to County Kerry, Ireland, to visit with relatives on the Casey and Healy farms of our grandparents.

"In a Time of Great Disorder" references Hester Prynne, a central character treated as an outcast in Hawthorne's 1850 novel *The Scarlet Letter*. The poem shifts to encompass others who relocated to places where they experienced discrimination. This includes many Irish after The Great Irish Famine and, in recent times, millions fleeing countries like Syria and Guatemala. The poem's title was inspired by a painting by the American artist Joan Snyder.

"River Force" recounts the death of an ancestor, Paddy O'Brien. Details came from a cousin, Sheila (Brounlie) Watson, who received them from her aunt Sheila O'Brien, who in turn received them from her aunt Bridget O'Brien. In the poem, the tavern and the men's conversations have been imagined. The term Samhain (SAH win) in the first stanza refers to the Gaelic festival marking the end of harvest season.

"Side Trip to Ballylee" was written after a visit to Thoor Ballylee, the tower in Galway that W. B. Yeats bought and restored to use as a summer retreat for his family. For Yeats, the tower held many meanings, which he sets forth in letters and in poems such as "Phases of the Moon," "A Dialogue of Self and Soul," and "Blood and the Moon." It was a symbol of his work, an emblem of the artist's aspiring creative force, and of night and a spiritual reality. With its once ruined top, the tower also became emblematic of dying nations. In *The Identity of Yeats* (Oxford University Press, 1964, p. 148), literary critic Richard Ellmann writes that Yeats embraced the often competing meanings as symbolic of man's own variability.

About the Author

Kathleen Aponick, a native of Cambridge, Massachusetts, has worked as an educational textbook editor and as a schoolteacher in Massachusetts and on a U. S. Army Post in Würzburg, Germany. She received an MFA from the Warren Wilson College Writing Program in North Carolina in 1989. Her poetry collection *Bright Realm* (Turning Point, 2013) was a finalist in the New Rivers Poetry Competition at Minnesota State University. She has also published two poetry chapbooks: *Near the River's Edge* (Pudding House Publications, 1995) and *The Port* (Finishing Line Press, 2006), which was named a Best Book of 2006 by *Monserrat Review.* Along with Paul Marion and Jane Brox, she co-edited *Merrimack, A Poetry Anthology* (Loom Press, 1992), a selection of poems written by poets who have lived along the Merrimack River in Massachusetts and Southern New Hampshire. Her poems have appeared in many journals, including *Notre Dame Review, Poetry Ireland Review, The Classical Outlook,* and *Poetry East.*

Made in USA - North Chelmsford, MA
1080897_9781950462797
04.20.2020 1349

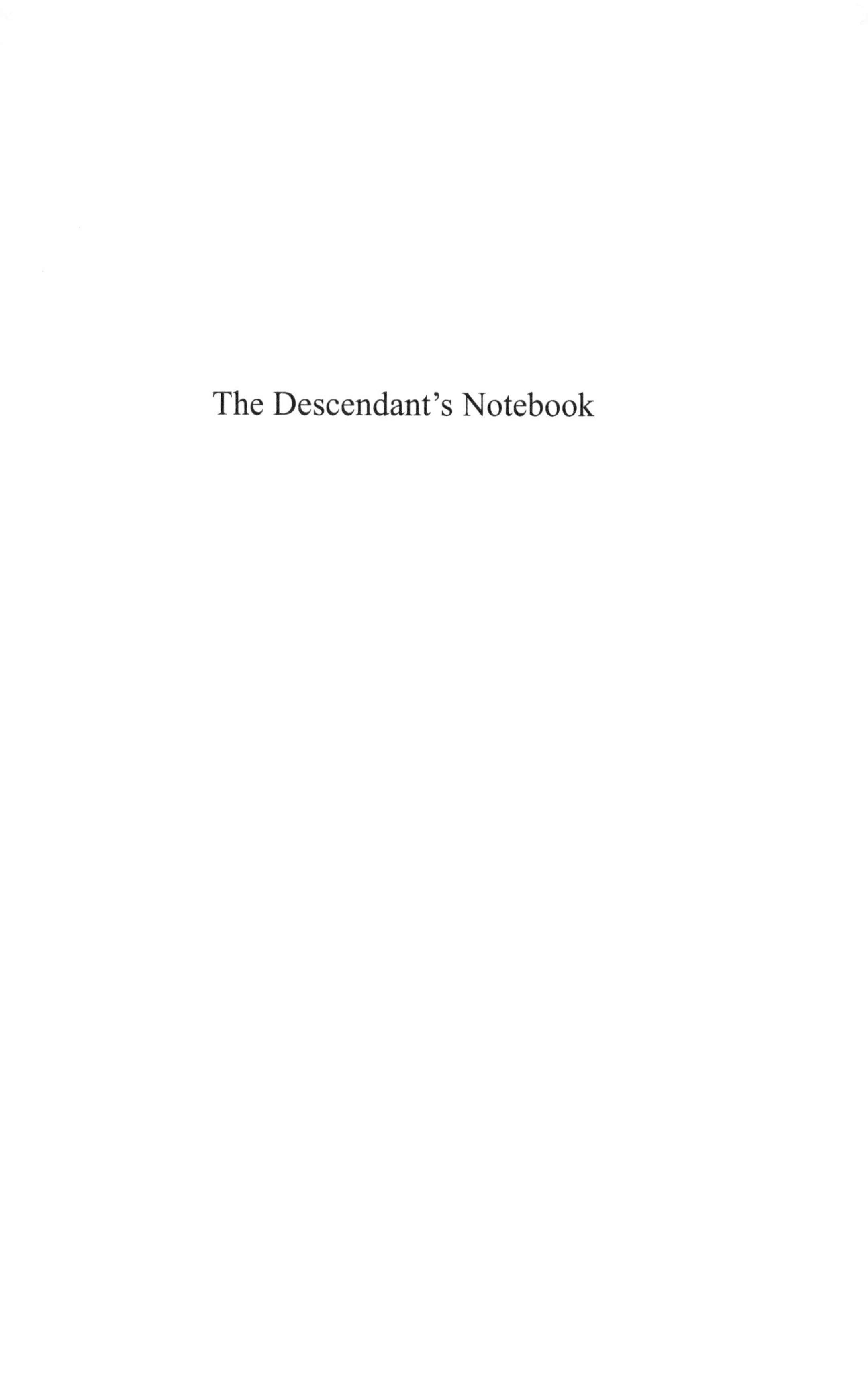

The Descendant's Notebook

The Descendant's Notebook